For George, Andrew and Bloom

Westonbirt Arboretum's

TREE SPOTTER'S GUIDE

The Definitive Guide
to Britain's 100 best trees

Dan Crowley

EBURY
PRESS

3 5 7 9 10 8 6 4

Ebury Press, an imprint of Ebury Publishing,

20 Vauxhall Bridge Road,
London SW1V 2SA

Ebury Press is part of the Penguin Random House group
of companies whose addresses can be found at global.
penguinrandomhouse.com

 Penguin
Random House
UK

Design copyright © Ebury Press 2017

Text copyright © Dan Crowley 2017

Dan Crowley has asserted his right to be identified as the author
of this Work in accordance with the Copyright, Designs and
Patents Act 1988

Illustrations by Louise Morgan

Design by Small Dots

Project editor: Lydia Good

First published by Ebury Press in 2017

www.eburypublishing.co.uk

A CIP catalogue record for this book is available from the
British Library

ISBN 9781785036002

Printed and bound in India by Replika Press Pvt Ltd

Penguin Random House is
committed to a sustainable future
for our business, our readers and
our planet. This book is made
from Forest Stewardship Council®
certified paper.

Introduction

One of the best things about trees is that, generally, they don't move. Once you have found them you can go back to see them any time you like (unless they are on private land!). And trees are everywhere! Some of the best ones turn up in the most unlikely places. Any walk can become ten times more interesting once you really start looking at the trees; revealing a world of intricate details that can turn into a source of constant fascination.

So go on, take a closer look and see how many you can spot! You never know where it might take you or what you might find, so keep your eyes open and never stop looking.

Contents

Monkey Puzzle
Araucaria araucana

Nothing else looks quite like a monkey puzzle tree. It has overlapping, spiny, rigid leaves on sweeping branches. The cones are round and disintegrate while on the tree. The swollen base of old trees is akin to an elephant's lower leg. Lower limbs are lost with age and large trees are often features of small front gardens that they have rather outgrown.

Found in: *parks, gardens*
Origin: *Chile*

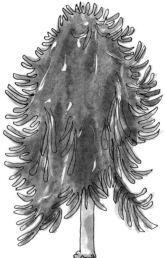

Yew

Taxus baccata

Common in churchyards, the yew is our oldest living tree. Some are reputed to be over 5,000 years old! It has short, thin, arching leaves neatly arranged along the shoot and will form a large rounded crown if not shaped or pruned as a hedge, as is commonly seen. Its berrylike fruit ripens red and this, excluding the seed within, is the only part of the tree that is not poisonous.

Found in: *churchyards, woodland, parks*
Origin: *Europe, North Africa, Western Asia*

Grand Fir

Abies grandis

The grand fir is one of the tallest-growing trees in Britain. The needlelike leaves are spread flat, sometimes drooping on either side of the shoot. Its small cones sit upright on branches high up in the tree.

The grand fir belongs to a group of trees known as 'true firs'. The leaves of true firs are needlelike and when pulled off leave the shoot smooth.

Found in: *forests, gardens*
Origin: *Western North America*

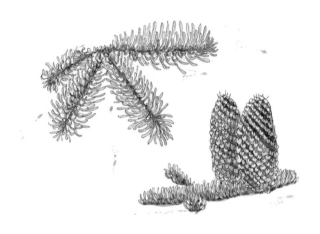

Noble Fir
Abies procera

The noble fir has distinctly blue foliage that is densely set along the upper side of the shoot. The cones can be very large and can be found on the upper branches of the tree.

As with all true firs, the cones sit upright on the branches and often disintegrate while on the tree. It is rare to find fallen fir cones fully intact.

Found in: *forests, gardens*
Origin: *Western North America*

Douglas Fir
Pseudotsuga menziesii

This tree has needlelike leaves that are similar to those of the true firs. It is easily distinguished from these by its single, slender, brown terminal buds. The cones are often found in abundance beneath trees and have protruding three-pronged bracts that are instantly recognisable. Trunks are often large with deeply fissured bark.

Examples of this species are the tallest trees in the British Isles.

Found in: *forests, parks, gardens*
Origin: *Western North America*

Cedar

Cedrus

Cedars are often found taking pride of place aside mansion houses and in larger gardens. They come in various shapes, colours and sizes and can be very large. They can be weeping, blue or spreading, and can be rather upright when young. They have mini barrel-like cones and evergreen foliage in rosettes on side shoots and singularly around the stem on branch tips.

Found in: *parks, gardens*
Origin: *North Africa, Asia*

Larch

Larix

Larches are one of five types of deciduous conifer. Before they shed their leaves in autumn they put on a fantastic display of yellow-gold colour. The needlelike leaves grow singularly around the shoot at branch tips and in rosettes on older wood, similar to those of the cedars. The cones are small and remain intact on the branches for some time but can also be found on the ground beneath.

Found in: *forests, parks, gardens*
Origin: *Europe and Asia*

Western Hemlock

Tsuga heterophylla

The western hemlock has short, narrow leaves of various length, which are scattered around the shoot. Some are upturned, revealing the whitish stripes that are found on the underside. Cones are small and hang from the tips of shoots and may also be found in abundance beneath the tree. Often used as a forestry tree, plantations are noticeably dark and are home to few other plants.

Found in: *forests, parks, gardens*
Origin: *Western USA*

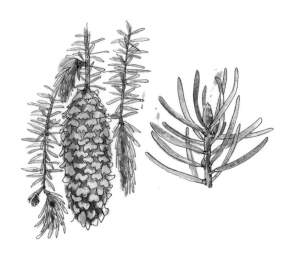

Norway Spruce
Picea abies

Spruces are easily distinguished by their hanging, bractless cones and their needlelike leaves which are attached by small, woody pegs.

Commonly used as Christmas trees (including in Trafalgar Square), the Norway spruce has dark green to grey-green leaves that point forwards and sideways above the shoot. Bark can be reddish when young but grey and somewhat scaly on older trees. Cones ripen orange-brown and are sometimes as large as this book!

Found in: *forests, parks, gardens*
Origin: *Northern Europe*

Serbian Spruce

Picea omorika

One of the easiest to identify from a distance, the Serbian spruce has a very tight, spire-like form, with down-curving, sweeping branches. The needles are green on the outside and have two waxy white stripes on the inside. Its cones are around a third of the size of Norway spruce cones.

The distinct form is believed to be an adaptation to reduce snow damage in its native range in Serbia.

Found in: *parks, gardens*
Origin: *Balkan Peninsula*

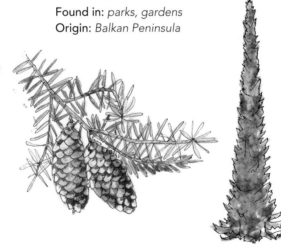

Colorado Spruce

Picea pungens

This spruce often has impressively silvery-blue foliage, though sometimes this vibrant colouring is restricted to the new growth. The needles are stiff, sharply tipped and spread upwards and forwards along the shoot. It is grown in a number of different forms, from traffic-cone shaped to compact and much in-between.

Found in: *parks, gardens*
Origin: *Western USA*

Sitka Spruce
Picea sitchensis

A close encounter with a Sitka spruce is unlikely to be forgotten. The dark green/blue-green needlelike leaves are sharp enough to warn against getting too close. Its smallish cones are pale brown and far more friendly.

It is fast growing and has long been a forestry favourite for difficult growing conditions. It can attain very large proportions and makes an impression as a single specimen.

Found in: *forests, parks, gardens*
Origin: *Western USA*

Black Pine

Pinus nigra

Pines are the largest group of conifers. Many different types are found in parks and gardens, as well as being grown for forestry. They have needlelike leaves which are usually held in bundles of two to five.

The black pine has grey-green needlelike leaves in bundles of two. The bark can be rough or scaly and often has a purple tinge. It can grow exceptionally large, sometimes with multiple trunks.

Found in: *forests, parks, gardens*
Origin: *Europe*

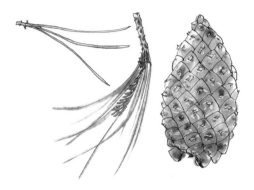

Monterey Pine
Pinus radiata

The Monterey pine is notable for its chunky cones which make a considerable thud when they fall. In its restricted native range in parts of California and Mexico, the scales only open after forest fires. It has bright green needlelike leaves held in groups of three. The bark of mature trees is purple-black and is very deeply fissured. Trees gain considerable size in next to no time.

Found in: *forests, parks, gardens*
Origin: *Western USA*

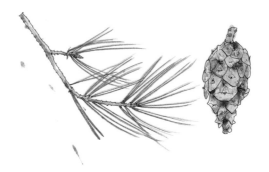

Scots Pine
Pinus sylvestris

This is the only species of pine native to Britain. It is easily distinguishable from a distance by the near salmon-pink bark in the upper crown. There are few things that look better than this against a clear, morning sky. The needles are held in groups of two, are slightly twisted and have a blue tinge. It rarely gets as large as the black pine.

Found in: *forests, parks, gardens*
Origin: *Europe*

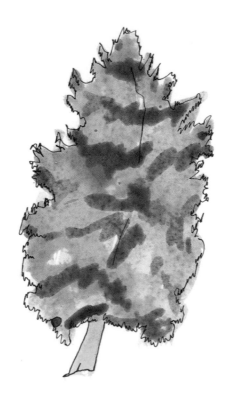

Bhutan Pine
Pinus wallichiana

The Bhutan pine has needles in bundles of five, which can be a dull green to almost blue. These tend to droop down and are sometimes kinked near the base. Resinous cones appear green on the tree before turning brown. They can be long and are slightly curved. It's not encountered as often as other species of pine, but it's no less significant and very elegant.

Found in: *parks, gardens*
Origin: *Himalayas*

Common Juniper
Juniperus communis

One of three native conifer species to Britain, the common juniper attains only small tree status. It has small, prickly, needle-shaped leaves in whorls of three that are green on the outside and bluey white on the inner surface. The berrylike fruits that are dark blue when ripe are used to flavour gin.

It has a native range larger than any other conifer and many different forms are grown in gardens.

Found in: *downland, parks, gardens*
Origin: *North America, North Africa, Europe, Asia*

Lawson Cypress

Chamaecyparis lawsoniana

Cypress trees have spray-like foliage, made up of small, scale-like leaves that overlap. Those of a typical Lawson cypress are blue-green on the upper side, with fine, waxy lines forming Y-shaped patterns beneath. The cones are small and round, with eight scales each.

A popular hedging plant, Lawson cypress will form a tree of considerable stature if given the chance. There are many varieties, which can appear very unlike each other!

Found in: *parks, gardens*
Origin: *Western USA*

Leyland Cypress

x *Cuprocyparis leylandii*

One of our most commonly encountered trees, though predominantly as an incredibly fast-growing evergreen hedge. It is a favourite for birds seeking somewhere to nest.

The leaves are small and scale-like, overlapping to form foliage sprays. There is little difference in colour of the underside of these sprays from the upper side, overall appearing a rather dull green.

Found in: *parks, gardens*
Origin: *a hybrid that occurred by chance in Wales*

Monterey Cypress

Cupressus macrocarpa

With upswept branches when young, that level with age to form a largely flat-topped tree, the Monterey cypress is similar to some cedars in form. The dense, somewhat lemon-scented foliage sprays and round fruit help to distinguish this species.

This is one parent of the hybrid Leyland cypress, with the other being the less frequent Nootka cypress.

Found in: *parks, gardens*
Origin: *Western USA*

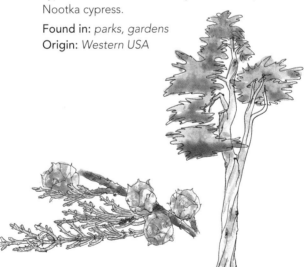

Western Red Cedar

Thuja plicata

The western red cedar has foliage similar to that of cypress trees but glossy, and handsomely so. It is also sweetly scented, some say it smells of pineapple. The underside of the foliage has broad whitish-green marks. It forms a large tree with swooping branches that will layer, if given the opportunity. The fruits are egg-shaped with tops that are spread open. It is also used for hedging, the scent unmistakable when cut.

Found in: *forests, parks, gardens*
Origin: *Western USA*

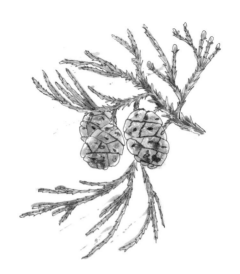

Giant Redwood

Sequoiadendron giganteum

These are the world's largest trees by volume. It has scale-like leaves that are short and pointed but is most noted for its very thick and spongy bark. Its cones are small and round; perhaps not quite what you might expect from such a large tree. Like the coast redwood, it hails from California, a hotbed of huge conifers. Many of the world's biggest trees come from the west coast of North America.

Found in: *parks, gardens*
Origin: *Western USA*

Coast Redwood

Sequoia sempervirens

In its native range in California, coast redwoods are the tallest trees in the world and grow for thousands of years. However, the oldest trees in Britain are less than 200 years old. The foliage is similar to yew, but has distinct white stripes on the underside. The tree has very thick bark like the giant redwood (but more spongy) and like many conifers, grows very upright.

Found in: *parks, gardens*
Origin: *Western USA*

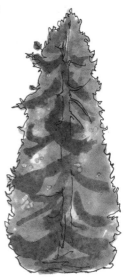

Japanese Red Cedar

Cryptomeria japonica

The small leaves loosely resemble those of the giant redwood but are larger and angled further away from the shoot. Unlike the giant redwood, it has hard, stringy bark and the cones are round with small hooks. Numerous varieties are grown in gardens, and some appear rather unlike the typical form!

Found in: *forests, parks, gardens*
Origin: *Japan*

Swamp Cypress
Taxodium distichum

The swamp cypress grows wild in and near swamps where it produces remarkable 'knees' that protrude from the ground near the base of the trunk and can be over a metre high. It often does the same in Britain when grown near water but, in drier conditions, these unusual growths are absent. Notable for its golden autumn colour, this deciduous conifer arranges its leaves alternately.

Found in: *parks, gardens*
Origin: *Eastern USA*

Dawn Redwood

Metasequoia glyptostroboides

The Dawn Redwood, another one of the deciduous conifers that puts on a show in autumn, was discovered in 1941 in China, having previously been considered long extinct. It is now an often-seen tree in larger parks and gardens.

The shoots and leaves are arranged in opposite pairs along the stem, helping to distinguish it from the swamp cypress. Shaped like a traffic cone, it grows impressively tall.

Found in: *streets, parks, gardens*
Origin: *China*

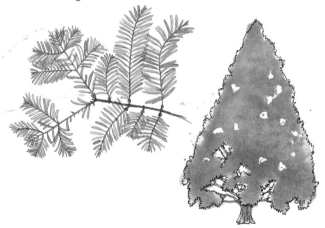

Maidenhair Tree

Ginkgo biloba

An extraordinarily resilient tree, the maidenhair tree has been around since the age of the dinosaurs. Although endangered in the wild, it is widely grown in town parks and gardens. It tends to grow slowly, with a narrow shape particularly when young.

The leaves are uniquely fan-shaped and sometimes indented. Though the leaves are broad, the tree is more closely related to the conifers than broadleaved trees.

Found in: *streets, parks, gardens*
Origin: *China*

Golden Weeping Willow

Salix x *sepulcralis*

Often found growing close to water in parks and gardens, the weeping willow is distinctive for its drooping shape and shiny green foliage. In winter the gold to green slender shoots are a stand-out feature.

With roots that spread far and wide, willows tend to be fast growing. They are a source of aspirin, which is used as a painkiller.

Found in: *parks, gardens*
Origin: *A hybrid that occurred before the 20th century. Exactly where is unclear.*

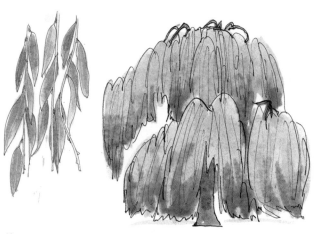

White Willow

Salix alba

The main trunk of white willow is often short, splitting into a number of stems that grow upwards at a steep angle, with branches that droop at the tips. The silvery, very slender leaves have silky hairs on both sides in spring, retained on the underside throughout the growing season. Often seen along rivers, the distinctive foliage helps to identify it from a distance.

One type of white willow is used to make cricket bats.

Found in: *wetlands, riverbanks*
Origin: *Europe, Western Asia*

Crack Willow

Salix x *fragilis*

The crack willow can be found growing with white willow but has a crown with wide-spreading branches and tips that do not droop. The leaves are also darker than the white willow and glossy, but pale beneath. However, it is important to note that willows are experts at crossbreeding and the crack willow is well known to cross with the white willow…identification can be tricky!

Found in: *wetlands, riverbanks*
Origin: *A hybrid with European and Caucasian parents*

Goat Willow

Salix caprea

The leaves of the goat willow are generally oval-shaped with a wavy or toothed outline, though this does vary. They have a leatherlike texture on the upper surface and are greyish and hairy on the underside. It tends to be a small tree and is distinctive for the plump catkins that appear in abundance before the leaves in spring.

Found in: *woodland, scrubland, gardens*
Origin: *Europe, Western Asia*

White Poplar

Populus alba

The white leaf undersides that are apparent even in the slightest of breezes help distinguish white poplar. The leaves are lobed, with those at branch tips more so than others. White hairs that create its distinctive appearance are also found on the new shoots. The bark is often fissured near the base, while there can be suckers nearby.

Found in: *streets, parks, gardens*
Origin: *Europe, Asia*

Hybrid Black Poplar

Populus x *canadensis*

This tree is a cross between the European black poplar and the North American eastern cottonwood and like many hybrids is fast growing. Trees can be extraordinarily large and are sometimes slanted. It has roughly triangular leaves with toothed edges and often has one or two small glands on the leaf stalk. The bark is fissured and trunks can be gigantic.

Found in: *parks, gardens*
Origin: *A hybrid that occurred by chance in Europe*

Grey Poplar

Populus x *canescens*

The grey poplar is a hybrid between the white poplar and the aspen. Like both of these, it produces suckers. It generally looks more like the white poplar, but it differs by its more rounded leaves that are grey underneath and less hairy. It also makes a bigger tree than both of its parents. All three turn a good yellow in autumn.

Found in: *parks, gardens*
Origin: *A hybrid that is first thought to have occurred in Europe*

Lombardy Poplar

Populus nigra 'Italica'

A very narrow shape with upright branches suggests Lombardy poplar, even from a distance, as there are few other trees that grow this way. The leaves are roughly triangular and similar to those of the hybrid black poplar but usually slightly smaller and without glands on the leaf stalk. It is often seen grown in lines along field boundaries, where it is planted to form a windbreak.

Found in: *field edges, parks, gardens*
Origin: *Widespread in Europe, thought to have originated in Asia*

Aspen
Populus tremula

Roughly round leaves with rounded teeth help separate this from the poplars. Though the leaves have hairs in spring, these are soon lost. It also produces suckers that, as with other types of trees, can have rather differently shaped leaves.

Aspen and the poplars are some of our noisiest trees. Their leaves flap and rustle in the slightest breeze so they are often heard before they are seen.

Found in: *woodland, parks, gardens*
Origin: *Europe, Asia, North Africa*

Silver Birch
Betula pendula

The silver birch has a slender shape with weeping branch tips. The bark is white higher up and with age can be thick, corky and fissured at the base. Black diamond shapes can also be found on the trunk. The brown shoots have white warts and the leaves can be almost triangular to rhombic in shape. Catkins appear over winter, enlarging in spring.

Weeping forms may also be seen.

Found in: *streets, woodland, parks*
Origin: *Europe, North Asia*

Downy Birch
Betula pubescens

Somewhat similarly barked to silver birch, though never as thick and corky, downy birch also lacks the diamond shapes on the trunk that are a feature of the silver birch. The shoots also have less warts (sometimes none), are hairy and the leaves are generally rounder. The characteristics of both of these species vary, though downy birch tends to have a less graceful overall shape.

Found in: *woodland, parks, gardens*
Origin: *Europe, North Asia*

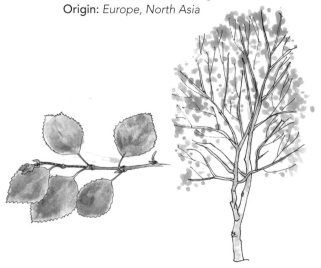

Hornbeam

Carpinus betulus

Hornbeam used to be known as hardbeam and for good reason: the wood is very hard. The trunk has muscle-like ripples, suggestive of the tree's strength. It produces catkins in spring and has toothed, oval-shaped leaves with impressed veins. The fruit that surrounds the small seed has three-lobed bracts. These often hang in abundance from the tree in autumn.

Found in: *woodland, streets, parks*
Origin: *Europe, Western Asia*

Elm

Ulmus

The leaves of elms are distinctly uneven at the bases and rough to the touch. Their green flower clusters appear in early spring, before the leaves emerge. Their seeds are enclosed in small, disc-like fruits.

Elms are less rare than some might think. Dutch elm disease has restricted many of them to growing in hedgerows but others have so far escaped and are an almighty size.

Found in: *woodland, hedgerows, parks*
Origin: *Europe*

Common Hazel

Corylus avellana

Common hazel tends to be a multi-stemmed shrub but can attain tree-like stature. Its catkins are visible in autumn and winter, enlarging before roughly rounded leaves emerge on hairy shoots. It produces hazelnuts, though those growing in woodlands tend mostly to be snaffled away by squirrels, for whom these are a favourite food.

Found in: *woodland, hedges*
Origin: *Europe, North Africa, Western Asia*

Turkish Hazel

Corylus colurna

Thanks to its ability to grow almost anywhere, Turkish hazel is often seen growing as a street tree. It has an oval crown that can be dense with branches, and bark that becomes corky. Catkins are produced in spring and the leaves are slightly lobed and heart-shaped at the base. Not always produced, its bizarre-looking, spidery fruit is an eye-catching sight in late summer.

Found in: *streets, parks, gardens*
Origin: *South east Europe, western Asia*

Italian Alder

Alnus cordata

Glossy, heart-shaped leaves and cone-like fruit help identify Italian alder. These fruits develop from catkins that appear in late winter to early spring. Its sometimes slender form lends itself to use as a street tree, where it shows resilience to difficult growing conditions.

Found in: *streets, parks, gardens*
Origin: *South Italy, Corsica*

Common Alder

Alnus glutinosa

Often seen growing in abundance close to rivers and streams, the common alder likes a drink! It has very round leaves with a wavy margin and often an indented tip. The fruit is a small (smaller than Italian alder) woody cone. In winter it is particularly distinctive as its stalked buds and catkins create a purplish haze.

Found in: *riverbanks, parks, gardens*
Origin: *Europe, Western Asia, North Africa*

Small-leaved Lime
Tilia cordata

The leaves of the small-leaved lime are roughly round with toothed edges, a pointed tip and a heart-shaped or flattened base. The underside can be slightly blue and has tiny tufts of gingery hairs. In the summer it can be totally covered in flowers that are loved by bees. You can often hear them as you approach the tree! The fruits are lemon-shaped or round.

Found in: *parks, gardens*
Origin: *Europe*

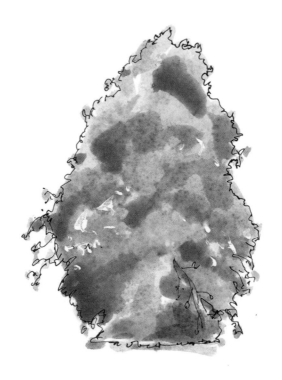

Common Lime

Tilia x *europaea*

A tendency to produce masses of sprouts on the trunk sets the common lime apart from many other trees. This provides great nesting spots for birds, though not all have this character. Its leaves are slightly bigger than the small-leaved lime and have hairs in paler tufts on the undersides. It is a favourite for avenue planting and fine examples can be seen in many areas.

Found in: *streets, parks, gardens*
Origin: *Europe*

Weeping Silver Lime

Tilia tomentosa 'Petiolaris'

One of the most beautiful of trees found in parks and gardens, the weeping silver lime is a joy to behold. It gets very large and its weeping branches hold leaves that have very long stalks and silvery undersides. Its flowers are toxic to bees and in summer many can be found beneath trees in a rather dozy state. The fruits are shaped like tiny peeled tangerines.

Found in: *parks, gardens*
Origin: *A form of unknown origin. The species is from south east Europe and western Asia*

Katsura

Cercidiphyllum japonicum

This tree can be distinguished by its oppositely arranged, circular and sometimes heart-shaped leaves that have rounded teeth. These emerge in beautiful shades of pink and orange in spring but they are most notable for their sweet nose-tingling scent from August through autumn that wafts through the air nearby. Katsuras are equally worth sniffing out for their autumn colour.

Found in: *parks, gardens*
Origin: *Japan, China*

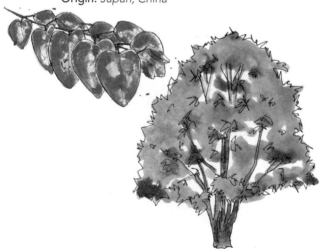

Persian Ironwood

Parrotia persica

The Persian ironwood has oval- to pear-shaped, wavy-edged leaves that colour spectacularly in autumn. It often takes a multi-stemmed form but can also be found growing on a single trunk. When visible, the flaky bark is attractively patchworked, similar to plane trees. The name ironwood relates to its particularly hard wood.

Found in: *parks, gardens*
Origin: *Caucasus*

Saucer Magnolia

Magnolia x *soulangeana*

Saucer magnolias are a common sight in suburban gardens. Its showy pink flowers appear in spring and sometimes again in autumn. The leaves are oval-shaped with a slightly pointed tip. In late winter the big, fluffy flower buds stand out, indicating how good a performance it will put on the following spring.

Found in: *parks, gardens*
Origin: *A hybrid that arose in a garden in France*

Bull Bay
Magnolia grandiflora

Bull bay has glossy, evergreen foliage that can be beautifully golden-coloured on the underside, though this can vary. Its large flowers are creamy white and appear dotted around the crown in late summer. Often seen growing against walls or close to buildings, it can also be found growing on streets and in gardens.

Found in: *streets, parks, gardens*
Origin: *Southeastern USA*

Common Holly

Ilex aquifolium

When used for hedging and regularly pruned, the common holly has sharply-spined leaves. On the upper branches, the leaves have practically no spines, except for a single one at the tip. The leaves are shiny and glossy on the upper surface and less glossy and slightly paler beneath. Red berries mature in autumn and may be held through winter.

Found in: *streets, parks, gardens*
Origin: *Europe, North Africa, western Asia*

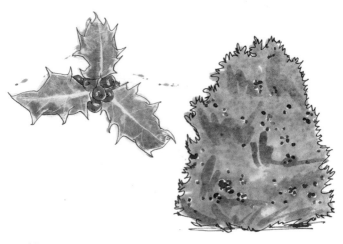

Box
Buxus sempervirens

Though often grown as a hedge or as a neatly pruned ornamental shrub, given long enough box can make a tree. The small, evergreen leaves are arranged oppositely and are often rather curved. The heavy, hard wood is sought after by woodworkers for making chess pieces, among other things. It is the only native tree with wood so dense that it does not float.

Found in: *parks, gardens*
Origin: *Europe, North Africa, Western Asia*

Common Beech

Fagus sylvatica

Common beech stands sentinel in many of our parks and gardens. Given space, it can have huge-spreading, swooping boughs and in woodlands it will grow taller than most other trees. It has oval-shaped leaves, fringed with hairs, that turn golden brown in autumn. Its inconspicuous flowers develop into husks that make a familiar crunch when trampled through in autumn and winter. Leaves are typically green, though there are many forms with deeper-coloured foliage.

Found in: *woodland, parks, gardens*
Origin: *Europe*

Common Oak

Quercus robur

Irregularly lobed leaves, with earlobe-like bases and acorns on long stalks, help identify this oak. The flower catkins in spring are often unnoticed. Good acorn years occur every two to five years.

Native to Britain, this tree supports more wildlife than most. It provides quality habitat for species of bird, insect, fungi and other plants. They also support many a treehouse! They are long-lived and suitably robust.

Found in: *parks, gardens*
Origin: *Europe, Caucasus, North Africa, Western Asia*

Sessile Oak

Quercus petraea

Our second native oak, the sessile oak, differs from the common oak chiefly in its stalkless acorns. The leaves are also more regularly lobed and are usually without earlobe-like bases. However, these two species can cross, producing trees with a mixture of characters.

A number of different galls can be found on our oaks. These are produced by trees as a result of an infestation by another being.

Found in: *parks, gardens*
Origin: *Europe, Western Asia*

Turkey Oak

Quercus cerris

Faster growing than either of our native oaks, the Turkey oak also reaches greater heights, eventually forming a humungous dome. Its bark is also more fissured than our native oaks; particularly apparent on massive trunks that often support huge boughs. Its leaves are lobed, often with teeth at the lobe tips. Its acorns have a mossy, furry cup and its buds are surrounded by whiskers.

Found in: *parks, gardens*
Origin: *Southern Europe, Western Asia*

Holm Oak
Quercus ilex

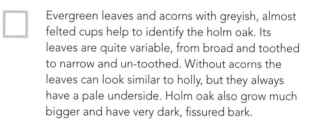

Evergreen leaves and acorns with greyish, almost felted cups help to identify the holm oak. Its leaves are quite variable, from broad and toothed to narrow and un-toothed. Without acorns the leaves can look similar to holly, but they always have a pale underside. Holm oak also grow much bigger and have very dark, fissured bark.

Found in: *parks, gardens*
Origin: *North Africa, Southern Europe, Western Asia*

Sweet Chestnut
Castanea sativa

This tree attains a mighty size, living for several hundred years. With age, it often develops very distinctive swirly bark. The leaves are large and glossy with big teeth. The nut is enclosed in a spiny husk and, once removed from this husk and roasted, makes a particularly tasty snack on a cold winter's evening.

Found in: *woodland, parks, gardens*
Origin: *Southern Europe, North Africa, Western Asia*

Field Maple

Acer campestre

This is the only maple considered native to Britain. It can be found as a small tree in woodlands and often pops up in hedgerows. It is also a common garden choice.

The leaves are three- to five-lobed with a smooth, un-toothed margin and may be hairy on the underside. The leaf stem contains milky sap and twigs and small branches can be rather corky.

Found in: *woodland, hedges, parks*
Origin: *Europe, Caucasus and North Africa*

Japanese Maple

Acer palmatum

As the days get shorter in autumn Japanese maples light up our gardens with colour. It has small lobed leaves that have a toothed edge. Trees tend to be roundish in shape and reach only a modest size.

Maples can be distinguished by their oppositely arranged shoots, foliage and winged fruit, known as 'keys'. Most maples have lobed leaves, though some are un-lobed and others made up of three or more leaflets.

Found in: *parks, gardens*
Origin: *Japan, South Korea*

Norway Maple
Acer platanoides

As spring arrives on our suburban streets and parks, the pale green flower clusters of the Norway maple are often prominent, appearing before leaves emerge. The leaves are lobed with occasional teeth on each side. The leaf stem also contains milky sap. Norway Maples come in many colours, with variegated and deep purple-leaved forms often planted.

Found in: *streets, parks, gardens*
Origin: *Europe, Caucasus*

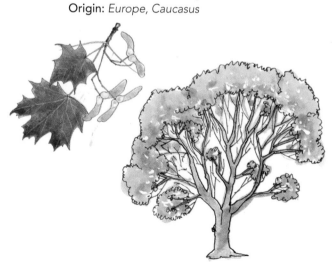

Sycamore

Acer pseudoplatanus

Though generally not considered to be native, sycamore behaves as if it is. Seedlings crop up nearly everywhere. Its lobed leaves often develop black spots later in the season, caused by a fungus that has a particular fondness for sycamore.

Forms with variously coloured foliage may be seen. Exceptionally eye-catching are those whose leaf undersides are purple; particularly beautiful when blowing in the breeze.

Found in: *woodland, streets, parks*
Origin: *Europe, Caucasus*

Silver Maple

Acer saccharinum

Silver maple has lobed leaves with jagged edges and a silvery underside. Tiny red flowers may be spotted high up in late winter, though this might be tricky as this maple can be large. The bark tends to be smooth and silvery grey. Trees grow vigorously, but the arching branches aren't to be trusted for climbing, as they are brittle.

Found in: *streets, parks, gardens*
Origin: *Eastern North America*

Sweet Gum

Liquidambar styraciflua

This tree has alternately arranged, lobed leaves that can appear almost star shaped. It is in autumn that this tree really stands out from the crowd, when the leaves turn spectacular shades of yellow, orange, red and purple. It can be confused with maples but the alternate leaf arrangement helps to distinguish it.

Found in: *streets, parks, gardens*
Origin: *Eastern USA*

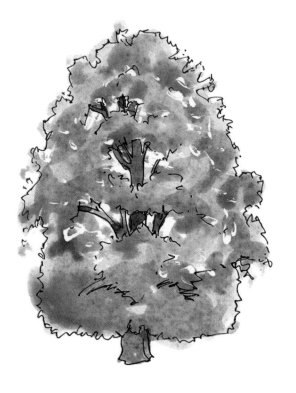

Tulip Tree
Liriodendron tulipifera

Tulip trees are large, with lobed leaves that are indented at the tip. Sometimes the side lobes are small and the indentation shallow, giving the leaf a slightly square outline. Its tulip-like flowers are produced in early summer, though often high in the crown, and being a greenish-yellow are sometimes tricky to spot against the leaves.

Found in: *parks, gardens*
Origin: *Eastern USA*

London Plane

Platanus x *hispanica*

This tree is distinctive for its large size and flaking patchwork bark. The leaves are similar to a maple but arranged alternately on the shoot. The fruits look like small balls, hanging in twos or threes.

Fantastic examples are found in city squares and parks. Its pollen can prove irritating but its resilience to urban conditions is admirable. It is the largest-growing broadleaved tree in Britain and the oldest-known trees haven't yet stopped.

Found in: *streets, parks, gardens*
Origin: *a hybrid that is thought to have arisen in England*

Oriental Plane

Platanus orientalis

A parent of the hybrid London plane, the oriental plane shares similarities with its offspring but differs in its deeper-lobed leaves, more weeping form, and fruits that tend to hang in chains of up to five or six. With a broad crown spread and ability to layer, the oriental plane can be at least as wide as it is tall.

Found in: *parks, gardens*
Origin: *Southern Europe, Western Asia*

Indian Bean Tree
Catalpa bignonioides

As confusing as it may seem, the Indian bean tree is from North America and not India. It has large, nearly round or sometimes lobed leaves that can have tiny black dots at vein junctions. The leaf stalk is hairless and the leaves omit a rather unpleasant smell when crushed. Candle-like flowers appear in summer and the fruit that develops from these are long, very thin, hanging pods.

Found in: *streets, parks, gardens*
Origin: *Eastern USA*

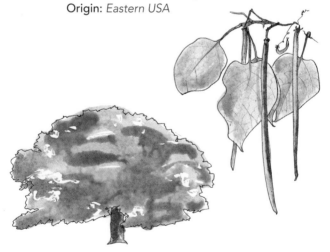

Foxglove Tree

Paulownia tomentosa

Foxglove trees have leaves that can be similar to those of the Indian bean tree but is easily distinguished by its hairy leaf stalk and hollow pith, apparent when a small shoot is cut through. The flowers are mauve and shaped like a foxglove flower. The seeds are held in large capsules that can remain on the tree for some time.

Found in: *parks, gardens*
Origin: *China*

Common Fig

Ficus carica

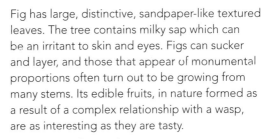

Fig has large, distinctive, sandpaper-like textured leaves. The tree contains milky sap which can be an irritant to skin and eyes. Figs can sucker and layer, and those that appear of monumental proportions often turn out to be growing from many stems. Its edible fruits, in nature formed as a result of a complex relationship with a wasp, are as interesting as they are tasty.

Found in: *parks, gardens*
Origin: *Western Asia*

Common Horse Chestnut

Aesculus hippocastanum

This tree can be very large, with huge swooping branches. It has big round leaves made up of (usually) seven leaflets. It has white flowers that stand candle-like throughout the crown.

Its conkers are the stuff of which playground dreams are made but their husks are covered in sharp spines.

It is distinctive in the winter due to its form and big, brown, sticky buds.

Found in: *streets, parks, gardens*
Origin: *Balkan Peninsula*

Red Horse Chestnut

Aesculus x *carnea*

This is a cross between the common horse chestnut and the American red buckeye. It is easily told apart from the common horse chestnut by its reddish flowers, smaller size, smaller leaves with usually only five leaflets and its not-so-sticky buds. The husks of its conkers also have less spines, or none at all.

The horse chestnuts come into leaf earlier than many other trees in spring, making them stand out from the crowd.

Found in: *streets, parks, gardens*
Origin: *a hybrid thought to have occurred, by chance, in Germany*

Indian Horse Chestnut

Aesculus indica

The Indian horse chestnut makes a large tree and has super-glossy leaves made up of usually seven leaflets that are larger than those of the common horse chestnut. The flowers also appear much later, meaning there is little mistaking the two. Its conkers are enclosed in dark brown spineless husks.

Found in: *parks, gardens*
Origin: *North West Himalayas*

Tree of Heaven
Ailanthus altissima

Reaching for the skies as fast as it can, the tree of heaven doesn't hang around for anyone.

Its huge leaves are made up of many leaflets, with glands on either side near the base. Flowers are produced in greenish clusters in summer and develop into keys that can be green or red before turning brown.

It grows admirably almost anywhere and often produces vigorous suckers that can pop up some distance from the original tree.

Found in: *parks, gardens*
Origin: *North China*

Common Ash

Fraxinus excelsior

A British native, the common ash is a large tree that has downward swooping branches with upturned tips. It has leaves made up of usually four to six pairs of leaflets and distinctive black buds. Its flowers are somewhat inconspicuous and its fruit are keys, produced in bunches. It is remarkable for its ability to change sex, either entirely or on single branches, on a regular basis.

Found in: *woodland, streets, parks*
Origin: *Europe, Caucasus*

Manna Ash

Fraxinus ornus

Unlike the common ash, the manna ash has showy flowers that are white and adorn mature trees in spring. Leaves are made up of five to nine variously shaped leaflets that are often more rounded than those of the common ash. Its buds are greyish brown.

All ashes have oppositely arranged leaves that are usually made up of leaflets of various shapes and sizes.

Found in: *streets, parks, gardens*
Origin: *Southern Europe, South west Asia*

Narrow-leaved Ash

Fraxinus angustifolia

Often seen in streets and a common choice of tree in town car parks, the narrow-leaved ash has leaves with usually seven to 13 pairs of narrow leaflets, as the name suggests. In contrast to typical common ash, it can turn attractive shades of orange, red and purple in autumn. It has dark brown buds that also help to distinguish it.

Found in: *streets, parks, gardens*
Origin: *Southern Europe, North Africa, south west Asia*

Black Locust

Robinia pseudoacacia

The typical black locust has leaves made up of several leaflets with un-toothed edges and clusters of white flowers, loved by bees, amongst green foliage in early summer. A variety with yellow leaves is also commonly seen. The fruit is a small pod and the trunk has deeply fissured bark and small, sharp thorns along some small branches. Black Locusts will also sucker.

Found in: *streets, parks, gardens*
Origin: *Eastern USA*

Honey Locust
Gleditsia triacanthos

Leaves of the honey locust are made up of several pairs of leaflets, or sometimes of leaves that are themselves branched. The main branches of the tree are sometimes viciously thorned, though one yellow-leaved form is entirely absent from thorns and so may be more desirable. They are generally small in stature.

Found in: *streets, parks, gardens*
Origin: *Central, Eastern USA*

Common Laburnum

Laburnum anagyroides

Common laburnum is generally a small tree that is relatively inconspicuous, aside from a few weeks in late spring when it produces spectacular chains of yellow flowers. These develop into pods that enclose the seeds, with both parts being poisonous. The leaves are made up of three leaflets that have a bluish underside.

Found in: *parks, gardens*
Origin: *Central, Southern Europe*

Black Walnut

Juglans nigra

Made up of several, often drooping, leaflets, the leaves of the black walnut are pleasantly scented and turn a beautiful yellow in autumn. Its nuts are round and hang on a short stalk…at least before the squirrels arrive.

Black walnut is one of the world's most valuable timbers and in the First World War was used to make aeroplane propellers.

Found in: *parks, gardens*
Origin: *Eastern USA*

Common Walnut

Juglans regia

Another favourite of squirrels, the common walnut is also the source of walnuts found on shop shelves and in kitchen cupboards. The tree itself has leaves made up of usually five to nine broad leaflets. It is also a valuable timber tree, used to make furniture.

Walnuts can be distinguished from a number of other trees by their chambered pith. Cut long ways, this appears similar to an upturned woodlouse. Wingnuts share this character.

Found in: *streets, parks, gardens*
Origin: *South east Europe, Asia*

Wingnut

Pterocarya

Wingnuts have leaves that are made up of many leaflets. They are particularly eye-catching for their fruit which are small, winged nuts that hang in long chains throughout the tree in late summer. A lover of water, they sometimes grow near lakes and streams in parks and gardens, though they can be found elsewhere. They are quick growing and some produce suckers that can crop up some distance from the main trunk.

Found in: *parks, gardens*
Origin: *Caucasus, Asia*

Elder
Sambucus nigra

A small multi-stemmed tree with leaves usually made up of five to seven leaflets, elder is well known for its flowers that are used to make a scrumptious cordial. The nearly black berries, held in large clusters in late summer and early autumn, can also be used to make crumbles and jam.

Found in: *woodland, scrubland*
Origin: *Europe, North Africa, Western Asia*

Rowan

Sorbus aucuparia

Rowan often stands out in late summer and early autumn, with its large clusters of deep red berry-like fruits that are swiftly taken by birds. The leaves are made up of several small, toothed leaflets and its flowers, though very attractive, have a particularly foul smell. Other rowans with orange fruit are also frequent, though these seem to be far less appealing to birds.

Found in: *woodland, parks, gardens*
Origin: *Europe*

Common Whitebeam

Sorbus aria

The common whitebeam has broad, thick oval leaves with prominent veins and toothed edges that are sometimes slightly lobed towards the tip and are whitish underneath. Flowers appear in clusters in spring and are followed by small, round, deep-red fruits in autumn.

As our native whitebeam, it can be found growing on chalky banks in parts of the country and is also commonly grown as a street tree.

Found in: *downland, woodland, streets*
Origin: *Europe*

Swedish Whitebeam

Sorbus intermedia

Swedish whitebeam has roughly oval-shaped leaves that are lobed in the bottom half and toothed towards the tip. The flowers are produced in clusters and the berry-like fruits are orangey red.

Whitebeams are sometimes grown on hawthorn rootstock, whose leaves can then cause confusion. They also often lean, as the hawthorn struggles to support its top.

Found in: *streets, parks, gardens*
Origin: *Europe*

Wild Service Tree

Sorbus torminalis

Infrequently encountered in parks and gardens, the wild service tree is an uncommon native that can be found in areas of ancient woodland. It has lobed leaves that are sometimes uneven with jagged tips. Its white fruit clusters develop into small, almost egg-shaped fruits that are brownish with orangey dots. It can be a bit of a looker in autumn, as the leaves turn almost golden.

Found in: *woodland*
Origin: *Europe, Western Asia, North Africa*

Wild Cherry

Prunus avium

Cherry blossom is one of the best sights in spring. White flowers adorn the branches of wild cherry trees as fresh leaves emerge. These leaves are oval-shaped with a toothed edge and often have a number of glands on the stalk. The fruits are red and enjoyed by birds. The bark is greyish purple, and shiny on young trees. It sometimes peels sideways, alongside distinctive brown bands that roughen with age.

Found in: *woodland, parks, gardens*
Origin: *Europe, Western Asia*

Cherry Plum

Prunus cerasifera

Purple-leaved forms of cherry plum are those most often seen, as they are commonly planted along our suburban streets. They have a scruffy appearance but their white or very pale pink flowers early in spring make it a joy nonetheless. The leaves are oval-shaped with a toothed edge and the fruits, rarely produced on purple forms, mature in late summer.

Found in: *streets, parks, gardens*
Origin: *Southern Europe, Western Asia*

Cherry Laurel

Prunus laurocerasus

Often a large multi-stemmed shrub, spreading wider than it is tall, the cherry laurel has long, shiny, evergreen leaves. In spring it produces attractive white flowers that develop into small, almost egg-shaped fruits that mature to nearly black. It is quicker growing than many trees and is often used as a hedge.

Found in: *parks, gardens*
Origin: *Eastern Europe, Southwest Asia*

Bird Cherry

Prunus padus

The bird cherry has oval-shaped leaves that, like those of the wild cherry, have glands on the leaf stalk. The pleasant-smelling flowers appear after the leaves in spring and like many of our trees are sources of nectar and pollen for wildlife. The fruits turn almost black when ripe and although they taste bitter to us, they are readily taken by birds, badgers and other mammals.

Found in: *parks, gardens*
Origin: *Europe, Asia*

Crab Apple

Malus sylvestris

Encountered mainly in woodlands and hedges, the crab apple has white flowers that emerge from pink buds in spring. It has small, oval-shaped leaves that have a toothed edge and its apples are small, yellowish green and very sour. Small branches have short spur shoots that often end with rather unfriendly thorns!

Found in: *hedges, woodland*
Origin: *Europe*

Ornamental Pear

Pyrus calleryana

A common choice as a street tree, the ornamental pear is usually seen with an upright shape. Its glossy, rounded leaves, with toothed edges and a pointed tip, often remain longer in autumn than many other species. Its white flowers come out with the leaves and its fruit are brown in colour, small and round to egg-shaped, with an indented base.

Found in: *streets, parks, gardens*
Origin: *China*

Common Pear

Pyrus communis

Flowering before the leaves emerge, the common pear can be one of our best spring performers. Its leaves are oval or rounded, with a rounded or slightly pointed tip. The fruits are (unsurprisingly) pear-shaped and appear in various sizes. The dark bark becomes fissured in small, nearly square shapes.

Found in: *orchards, parks, gardens*
Origin: *Caucasus, Asia*

Midland Thorn

Crataegus laevigata

Short thorns, dark green, lobed leaves and almost egg-shaped fruit containing two to three stones help identify the midland thorn. The typical form produces white flowers in May, contributing to the array of blossom on view at this time of year. They are generally small and often planted as a hedge in parks and gardens. Removing footballs from them can be tricky and painful!

Found in: *woodland, hedgerows, parks*
Origin: *Europe*

Common Hawthorn

Crataegus monogyna

The common hawthorn generally grows to a larger size than the midland thorn and has larger leaves with deeper lobes. Fruit is also rounder and contains just the one stone. It is also noticeably thornier! In appearance it can be somewhat variable and to complicate identification matters, the two also cross-breed.

Found in: *woodland, hedgerows, parks*
Origin: *Europe, North Africa, Western Asia*

Black Mulberry

Morus nigra

Mature black mulberries often have the appearance of being very old, with gnarled bark and a wide-spreading crown. The leaves are rough to the touch, usually oval, and un-lobed on fruiting branches but often very lobed on young growth. The fruit ripens to a deep purple-red and are edible straight off the tree, if you don't mind stained fingers.

Found in: *parks, gardens*
Origin: *Western Asia*

Cider Gum

Eucalyptus gunnii

Exotic-looking and very quick-growing, gum trees never take long to make an impression.

Gum trees have two distinct types of foliage: juvenile and adult. The juvenile foliage of the cider gum is round and the adult foliage oval-shaped or even narrower. Gum tree foliage frequently crops up in flower arrangements. They also often have spectacular peeling bark.

Found in: *parks, gardens*
Origin: *Australia*

Glossary

Bract A modified or specialised leaf

Catkin Usually drooping, tail-like flower head

Crown The tree's structural shape above the ground

Deciduous Losing its leaves in winter

Fissured Split or cracked

Gall A growth produced as a result of an infestation by another being; for example, a wasp or insect

Gland An area from where a substance is exuded

Hybrid The offspring of different types of tree that have cross-bred. Indicated by 'x' in the botanical name

Husk The outer covering of some fruits

Keys A winged fruit

Layer A branch that touches the ground, roots and produces another trunk

Leaflet A leaf-like part of a compound leaf

Lobe A projection on a leaf

Opposite Where leaves or leaflets are arranged in pairs, one each side of the stem

Pith The central part of a stem or twig

Rootstock A tree whose roots are used to grow another tree

Scale A tiny leaf, or the segments that form part of a cone

Shoot A young twig

Spur A short branchlet

Sprays Leaves arranged to form a fountain-like shape

Sucker A shoot growing from the base or root of a tree

Terminal The tip of a leaf or shoot

Whorl A circle of branches, leaves or flowers, produced from a single point

Acknowledgements

Thank you to:

Lydia Good and all at Ebury Press.

Louise Morgan for the amazing illustrations.

Mark Ballard, Andrew Smith and all at Westonbirt Arboretum for helping to make this happen. Special thanks to Susanna Byers, Matt Parratt and of course Emily Beaumont, without whom this book wouldn't be what it is.

Mum and Dad for your love and support. Gran and Grandad for your love of trees. Sarika for being here and The Gang at The Palace for being there.

The trees at Westonbirt and beyond. You are a constant source of inspiration.